Of One Mind

Myrtle Stedman

Sunstone Press
Santa Fe, New Mexico

HISTORY
First writing 1947
Published in 1974
Under the title, *OF ONE MIND*
Which is incorporated in this publication
Revised and expanded 1989

First Edition

Printed in the United States of America

Library of Congress Cataloging in Publication Data:

Stedman, Myrtle.
  Of one mind / by Myrtle Stedman. -- 1st ed.
      p.   cm.
  ISBN: 0-86534-155-9   : $10.95
  1. Stedman, Myrtle--Philosophy.   I. Title.
NA737.S637A2   1990a
191--dc20   90-46382
                                                       CIP

Published in 1990 by SUNSTONE PRESS
                 Post Office Box 2321
                 Santa Fe, NM 87504-2321 / USA

*Dedicated to the Children
and
to others to whom I am
indebted for help or
encouragement.*

TABLE OF CONTENTS

Automatic Writing

In the beginning was the Word
and the Word was with God,
and the Word was God.
The same was in the beginning
with God.
All things were made by him;
and without him was not anything
made that was made.
In him was life; and the life was
the light of men.
And the light shineth in darkness;
and the darkness comprehended
it not.
— ST. JOHN 1:1-5

Who or what
sits at the right
hand of God
enough to solve
the riddle
we have just read?

If in the beginning
was the Word,
then
in the beginning
was the
mind.

In what spirit did
it make
everything?

In what light
shall we comprehend
that which the darkness
did not?

Who will be so bold
as to take my pen,
push my hand;

to put before my eyes
a wiser thing
than I know?
Who can be so aroused;
who or what has something to say
through me?

If there is a group of spirits
standing around me,
is there not one
who will use my hand?
I give my hand — and my pen —
freely to one,
more learned than I;
one in a position
freed of opinion
because of pure knowledge,

Yet one who can see the advantage
of having a hand
and a piece of paper,
not for himself
but for me.
I have the pen,
I have the paper;
but I have no idea what to write.

I am a babe,
I am a lover,
I am an old woman.

There is a spirit within me,
as open to the light
as a flower.

I turn my head
this way and that,
the light itself directing me,

yet I know not how
to go in
or come out.

Who says, "We are not
supposed to ask
the things of God?"

I want to know,
everyone I know
wants to know.

Can automatic writing give us a clue
to why we are unknowing?

To tell us what the mind
surely knows
of life and death?

Or is this for us
to figure out;
the thing that must be
so obvious
to a mind that knows?

9

As the turtle dove calls from his space
to another in space,
I feel called
and am listening.
Or is it I who call
and they who listen?
Spirit is reciprocal
or nothing at all.

It takes two actions
to cause a spirit —
one expressive,
one receptive.

It's a moot question
which comes first.

There is energy
and there is no energy.
There is no energy
and there is energy.
This something
and nothing,
this nothing
and something,
is love.

There, and there,
is true correspondence.

10

It is in the space
between the
called and the listening
and the listening and the calling.
Even the dead respond in spirit.

I want to be in on the communication
between the living
and the dead.

What truth is waiting
to be known?

Who is willing to help
with this?

What is
his or her name?
How shall I call it?

Will it be a group consciousness,
speaking for the one mind
that knows everything?

Or as intimate as one to one,
just between the mind's own
expression and receptivity
in each one
of us?

Let us develop the subject
"Of One Mind."

Take my hand,
put the mind's power into it,
direct its passage over this sheet; let it
flow — let it go — let it
get to the depths and the heights.

Let me let go
of all that is gross,
all that has stood
in my way.

Open up my receptivity
like a lover
does without words.

I want to experience
a love — the love — of love;
the joys of joys of an intimate
feeling — the esthesis — of esthetics; the
spiritual discernment
that gives sense to sense.

I want this perfect exchange
with overwhelming assurance.

I want to break down all resistance,
all walls and doors,
all objections and doubts,
with a knowing that is pure.

I want to drink of the waters
withheld in the rocks,
of the sap in the trees
rooted to the ground;

I want to know and experience
the sure-footed esthesis of the goat,
the radar sensing of the bat.

I want the same guidance
as the migrating birds
and the bee for its hive.

I want to activate — wake up —
the slumbering mind.

I want to be able to say,
"Let it rain"— and see rain;
"be well," and see illness vanish.
Is this asking too much of the mind
that created all?

Did the mind ever create all?
Is it creating as we go along?

Is it us? Are we it?
The same that is in rocks
and trees and man?
In the whales
and the seals,
the porpoise
and the dolphins?

Use my hand,
use my pen,
open these wonders
to me.

I wait for the spirit
to move me.

I lie down like a puppy
to have my belly scratched.

I nibble at everything
and nothing.

I am full of expectancy.
Surely there is a spirit
that will throw me a stick.

14

I scratch in the dirt,
I roll in the grass,
I splash up and down
in the waters in the ditch.

Shall my owner
continuously say,
"No don't do that"?
What holds my pen
and keeps it from writing?

I'll bring back the stick
and lay it at your feet.

Just try me.
I am waiting.

Come
be with me —

Take my hand —
move my pen.

I want to know
what a spirit
can convey.

Should I be more specific?
All right, then —
I want to see the barriers dropped
between life and death.

I want to see death
out of the way.

Make me see
what I already
should know.

I am too much me.
I want to be
somebody else writing.

I want to see pure truth
before my eyes.

16

Are you telling me
that I must
look at a tree
to find truth;

that truth is obvious
to any observer;
to a feeling in a toe;

to a pain
in the neck?

Is all this automatic
with practice?

There is something about a person
that absolutely calls
for necessity;

it is the cause
before effect,

it is the dryness
before the rain,

the silence
before the outburst;
it is the human before the divine.

17

Of One Mind

19

I longed to know the mind,
and I knew it, and it knew me.

A progression of ideas filled my
successive longings,
a little at a time as
I was able to bear them.

Repeats and recurrences came as
repetition in a composition,
echoing one design.

The rhythm ebbed and flowed between
knowing and longing to know and rose to
a peak through the study of lowly things.

I wrote this to give form
to that which I know.

The universe seemed moved
by my longing.

A deep dark abyss opened before me
and I retreated with fear and trembling.

Then I saw a light reach out and return to
its beginning. And the abyss rose and fell
with this turning to and return and was
enlightened by the activity.

The light was shadowed
and there was form.

And the whole universe acknowledged the
consummation and rejoiced.

And I heard this saying, *Four stages lead to
wisdom and understanding.*
And I saw that the oneness of mind
and all of its forms is based on a love com-
mon to all.

TODAY — if you will —

*. . . . the Lord Himself shall give
you a sign; . . . .*
— Isaiah 7:14

Behold, a virgin shall conceive, ...
— Isaiah 7:14

Imagine if you can an infinite death-like before-time rest — virgin mind in semiconscious repose. Close your eyes and all is darkness as far as you can see. Watch, for there is a quickening and a flickering of light to be observed. Then rest again while you contemplate what you have seen. But look, for the darkness quickens again and light is at hand. She stirs with another quickening and sighs, and quickens again and again in a chain until it becomes a necessity for the light to possess her and she him.

And where she draws him she follows; so that there is a breathing increasing until it mounts to an agonized stillness. Then there is a blinding flash and an explosive declaration in the giving and the taking. After the recession and when there is again a period of rest, and change can be observed, there is light and darkness, divided, yet one. And the darkness is pregnant with form.

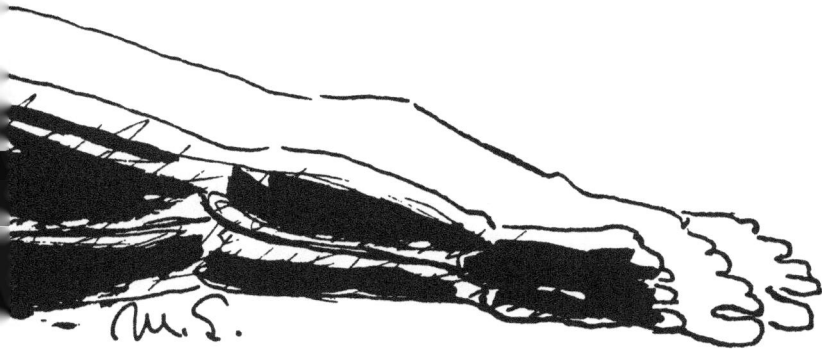

Except for the darkness of the mind longing for the light of the mind, there would be no beings visible in form, nor any tangible ideas separated from the intangible. All space is spaced and placed with forms of light and darkness. All forms are sensitive — and all are consciously motivated so that there is a prevailing spirit — a will and willingness to be and to *Let there be* multitudinous forms of the mind.

Light is the brilliance of the mind —
darkness gives it depth and form.

If there were all light, nothing could be
seen or understood. If there were all
darkness, nothing could be seen or
understood. The two together create the
image which can be seen and understood.

. . . . and bear a son,
— Isaiah 7:14

Cognizance

I saw that mind is the one constituent in its own constitutional power. It embraces and enlightens its own darkness, revealing the many shapes and forms that it takes and so makes.

We and all things are made in their image —
of the mind's own light and darkness —
the visual aspect of the consciousness born
by their love.

Consciousness is sustained in the mind's
activity.

All the variations of the mind's movements
make up our very complex world within
worlds, visible or invisible.

All expressive movements of the mind
move in relation to all receptive
movements the mind makes, so that it
always retains the character of its own
oneness.

The mind follows where it is drawn by mind.

The energy emanating from one movement is that which is received by the other movement, bearing likenesses of both the expressive and the receptive aspects of the mind in a multitude of variety.

Only the mind itself is involved in this infinity.

All that can be experienced is the expressed and conceived ideas of the mind and everything reveals the nature of the mind creating it.

In bearing the light, the role of the virgin
darkness should not be obscured.

For instance —
there slowly came a time when I
experienced the pages of a book, pages
appearing to be almost blank. I knew that
if I could completely accept the fact that
there was printing on the pages and
associate seeing with understanding I
could then say, *I see.*

I worked with this idea and I understood
the idea. Letter by letter began to appear
blacker and blacker, until I saw light and
darkness, in balance and of one accord.
This came about slowly, reversing on days
when I gave up the urge, which has its
own meaningful message: to be constant,
to do what one has been inspired to do.

. . . . *and shall call his name Immanuel.*
— Isaiah 7:14

Or, *Emmanuel, which being interpreted is, God with us. (Matthew 1:23)* This is the consciousness of our own position of oneness of mind.

We are continually reasoning together to realize this state of oneness of mind.

All ages have been more or less ages of reason, because reason is agitation, a restless condition. Reason is the unsettled motion of the mind.

Inspiration is the flash of light released at the point of agonized stillness, when the mind becomes completely receptive to the expressive nature of the mind.

Facts are the children of the agitated feelings which by mental reflection give life to the images of the mind.

I dedicated myself to the imagery; to seeing the mind in action without error or illusion.

I cast a thought as a tent over an orchard of fruit to protect it from hail, and it was protected.

I saw clouds gather together at my call; and I saw clouds and said to them *Be off,* and they disappeared. To say, *Be off* to clouds could cause a serious drought if it were not for others who could say, *Let it rain.*

I longed to know the mind and I knew it
and it knew me and set my fancy free.

Fancy is the imagination based on imagery.

When we dwell too much on facts already
established in the mind, the use of the
mind is restricted within the solidity of
these facts. This may be well, efficient, and
good if the oneness of mind is doing what
it wishes and what it has made up its mind
to continue to do. But here is the hope
and the established fact that we have
the power to change the things of our
doing simply by acknowledging the
presence of mind to do so.

This gives us the dominion and the
authority to say *Be gone* or to say
Gather together.

Twice I have been on very rough waters,
and I have said *Be calm* and instantly the
water was calm.

Likewise, a longstanding tic-douloureux left
an old gentleman and bothered him no
more.

In another instance a child's club feet
straightened when I put her down and
expected them to plant themselves firmly
on the ground and carry the child's weight.

I have been in cyclone and storm, and
have said *Lift up* or *Give way* and have
passed under or through without harm.
And I have done it for others far away
when I heard of their plight; and I heard
over the same means of communication
that the storm obeyed.

To know that the mind is universally one
puts us in contact with any one phase of
activity within it, that we know of, and
gives us a chance to call upon the mind to
give us only the facts of its true likeness
and being; and thus remove illusions out
of character to its oneness and love.

Many minds or even two minds, if there
could be such, would tear the oneness of
mind apart and its creative ability would be
lost. But this can not be.

The mind's whole nature is to be one.

. . . . I AM <u>THAT</u> I AM . . . .
— Exodus 3:14

This is an ideal universe, governed by what is uppermost in the mind. Fortunately, this is the mind's own consciousness of itself.

The more conscious we are of the mind, the more good we will see in living. There is freedom in the infinity of its scope and finite dynamics in the focalization of every idea reached to as an end. The idea becomes a reality to the receptive mind. If the reality changes with a change of mind, I know this —

the only unchanging reality is the mind's
own conception of itself.

. . . . *the light shineth in the darkness;* — but it should not be said anymore, *and the darkness comprehended it not.*
    — *St. John 1:5*

The darkness is the evidence of the receptive nature of the mind.

When I saw the dark abyss, I asked *What is the abyss?* And I heard *Open mind* and the abyss was promptly filled with light.

The open mind is the womb that gives form to that which it has come to know; and is the means of satisfying its own longings.

To know and be known of the mind is wisdom and understanding.

And the whole universe shares in the consummation.

Its image is the sign of the presence and oneness of mind.

In view of this light, the virgin darkness of the mind has lost none of its purity.

She was always, and is ever, the bride.

And he, the light, her bridegroom.

Our own identity can be placed with one or the other and then both, in the full consciousness of Being.

Mind discloses its own immaculate conception of itself — in love.

In love we bear witness to its love.

Channeling

53

What could be more
informative
than love?

The love of a father,
the love of a mother
is love.

The love you know
in your bed
is love.

Love is a spirit,
love is the spirit
between that which is loving
and that which is loved.

Love is the word
made flesh,
the writing on the page,
the babe in the manger,
the wind in the trees,
the murmur in the stream,
the frog in the pond,
the bark of the dog,
the wave of the ocean,
the work well done.

The love you remember
is as potent
as the love of today.
All is raised up
and risen
in love.

I lost a son
  who should not
    have died:
        unless . . . .

was there something
he accomplished?
Is there something in the future
his dying will do?

If we believe in the hereafter,
then there is no dying.

Will he come somehow
to prove that he lives?

Will he communicate
his presence?

If there is just one mind,
and we all have that mind
and he lives;
then surely
he should have no problem,
neither we,
whose ears strain to hear.

Is there a hearing deep within,
a reservoir of knowing —
some sign,
some feeling —
which will assure us,
without a doubt?

I want my son
to figure this out.
He was imaginative,
and a worker.
He didn't want to leave us.
It is his predicament;
he will find a way.

With such a mind as
        he entertained
                he may even
                        put the essence
                                of life
                                        back on their
                                                skeleton bones
                                                        for us.

He died with a vision,
        an image
                of himself —
        of being free
                to investigate the earth
and all the things he was curious about.

        He prepared for himself
                a new environment,
        a step forward;
                not backward,
                except to beckon
                        to us.

        Have we the open mind
                to follow
                        his find?

The mind is more virgin
than a forest;
more virgin
than pure olive oil.

Virginity is the open spaces
of the universal mind
filled only with
what we can
not see.

It is filled to the brim
with spirit;
with a give
and take attitude.

Take is the channel
through which
the mind
gives.

This activity
produces its own
cognizance of itself.

This is all the doing,
all the isness
that there is.

This cognizance says
"I am",
And in these two words
the whole presence of the mind exists.

"I am," constitutes
a body of mind,
a body as eternal
as that which makes it.

How then can we say
that we die?

We will never be
without a sense
of body.

The mind plays a game
of hide and seek
with us.

And I am "it", for the moment
standing at my post,
counting —
one, two, three, four, five,
six, seven, eight,
nine, ten — and up
to fifty.

All that are not ready
holler "I"
for I will seek you out
and find you.

Our father,
our mother,
our brothers
and sisters;
our husband and wife;
our son and grand —
and greatgrand —
children;
our cousins and
uncles and aunts ;
our pets and all that
we hold dear
or merely stumble upon, ad infinitum —

you shall appear
familiarly clothed
before my
spiritualized eyes.

But I shall run
to my base
and pat you in
before you
can get there.

There are always rules
to any game
worth playing.
And the rule here, is

to know
and be able to
recognize
those whom you
are seeking.
And
we have to seek them
where they are —
in the active
expression
and reception
of the mind.

I will illustrate —
my mother
stood by me
on a train
after her funeral
to see that I was
alright, as she
was used to doing
when I was a child.
I saw her.

My brother arose from
the solar plexus of the earth
in a cornucopia of white and blue light,
then descended a wide stairway
with his deceased bride;
and they sat on a park bench
arm in arm.
I saw them.

A friend told me,
"Myrtle, you know
I am not buried
in that box."
I knew that.

Another friend said,
"I tried to get back
into my body
but I just
couldn't make it."
I agreed.

Another—"Myrtle, <u>you</u>
know that I am
not dead."
"Yes, I know."

My husband said,
"If I possibly can
communicate with you
after I am gone,
I will." He did.

He appeared in a doorway —
both my dog and I
felt his presence and understood
that he wanted us to know
that he was there.

He had said, "If I live again
I would like to be a robin"—
because he admired them
so much.

He appeared as that bird
and chirped the message;
that was an ordinary
command that
I understand.

I saw my cat's spirit
rise above her prostrate form
in her own shape
and coloration;
I heard her meow
that night,
above her grave.
I was exceedingly glad
that she had made it.

I've lost all fear
of death;
it cannot
touch me or you.

My own son
stood beside my bed
and I said, "Hi, Tom",
and felt his
satisfied reaction.

Did you know
that life itself
is pure fun?

When I was a child
I sat on our
porch balustrade
and I visualized
a whole pile
of pennies;
a cone as high
as my head.

My Sunday school teacher
had told me
"All good is from God."

And all through my life
I've pondered this thought.

And I've given "Him" credit
for every penny
I've been given;
every one I've earned
or found on the ground.

And I've given
myself credit
for having an
open mind,
and for being able
to visualize;
to compile
and to collect mementoes
of this vision
of wealth
and abundance
that can be seen
in a day dream.

And I've always thought
that there is
more than just "Him."
There has got to be a
"Her" with "Him",
and now that
the smallest child
knows where
babies come from,
it is well past "due date"
for the rest of us to realize
that to give "Her" credit
brings back a balance to our lives.

Please tell your children
about Her
when you tell them
about Him.

She is the conceptual
frame of mind.

Her name is Grace.
She it is who materializes,
dematerializes and materializes
again and again
the circumstances
and the things of the spirit.

73

The Catalyst

75

Why would we seek anything
as long as we were satisfied?
What is the catalyst
that causes the seeking?
I could make a long list:
everyone on this list
screaming silently
or aloud
for change;
everyone on the list
good in themselves
because of this.
Make no mistake;
this is how it is.

There is fear,
there is depression:
there is a feeling of emptiness.
There is frustration,
hatred,
a negative attitude
seemingly everywhere.

Every one of us
could feel
suicidal
when things go all wrong
for us.
A terminal disease
is a more acceptable
way out.
A quick fatal accident
is a good way to go.

The primitive woman
who announces
"God has taken
my poor sick child"
is more right
than wrong.

Death is a provision
for change
which we have seen
no way of making.

We shoot and stab;
we burn down
and steal.
We would blow up
the earth —
to heck with it all.

We would drown ourselves
in our own tears.
But there comes a time
for every
one of us,
to feel a sense
of joy
for no reason at all;
every feeling takes
a turn about face.
It is an unmistakable happening.

The fear is all gone,
the depression
is turned to a tingling hope;
inspiration diffuses frustration,
hatred turns to an
overwhelming love;
negativity turns to a positive attitude,
a definite change
takes place:
there is no denying it.
The earth is gorgeous,
and
all people are just like us.

So what are we?
We are curious
at last —
God made manifest?

Impossible, you say,
though you know
deep within you
that it is so — how so?
And this is where we start
to realize that we live and breathe
and have our being in God.

Through a catalytic change
that completely shatters
the feeling of "simply being
bored to death,"
you live again though you were dead.

Curiosity brightens
our whole outlook.
When we are curious
about how the mind works,
it will tell us; and it will give us
evidence of itself
in concrete works.

We are its works
and have never been
anything else.
This is the mystery
of its own virginity.

Again,
have we not
heard and read
I am the Lord your God
and there
is none else, ...
— Isaiah 45:5

He
is speaking for
Her too,
and they are alive in
these words.

Remember,
it takes two words
to understand God.
I for the light
of the mind,
am for the darkness.

Except for the values
we find in the darkness,
we would be blinded
by the light.

Except for the
darkness of night
we could not see
the stars.

Are we not rested
and nourished
in darkness?

Though darkness
would shroud
herself in mystique,
we shall disrobe her.

Only by our knowing
will she stand
naked and unashamed —

that light
and darkness
are partners
in wisdom
and
understanding.

For dissatisfaction
we should be grateful,
if it brings us in our search
to the knowledge
that we are
of one mind
and in complete
cognizance
of what
this mind is.

83

Living by Grace

One day in meditation I heard,
"What you need is
more grace."
For years and years
I wondered
what this meant.

And now I know.
It is the ability
to be quiet,
to listen,
to be willing to love;
to watch with my eyes
what other eyes
tell me;
to use my ears
to hear a catch
in a breath;
to smell out the
scent of a body
passing by.

Don't let anyone tell you
you can not rely
on your physical senses.
What are senses
but the feelings
of the mind?

How could an artist paint,
an author touch you
with his or her writing,
if this were not so?

They have allowed their eyes
to see the invisible,
their ears to hear
the unhearable,
and their mind
to touch the unfeelable.

The archaeologist, the architect,
the builder
the inventor,
the woman baking a pie —
all materialize the
invisible.

The musician hears
the music
before it is written.

The mind
knows your need
before you are
conscious of it.
It is more conscious than you
and it puts you on the way
to realize its presence.

The lights will turn green,
the traffic will part
for your company,
the parking space
will be waiting, and the
doors will open for your
opportunity.

Only good can come
from this realization.
We cannot use it or
misuse it
or it will leave us
high and dry.
We simply observe it,
but definitely
deserve it.

It may take years of work —
but once you catch on
it does everything
for you, or paves the way,
for your work.

All it calls for is
a complete
involvement
in training your senses
to look for grace in Grace.

She is the Queen
of the Kingdom of Heaven
from whence . . . . *all these things*
shall be added unto you *—
as soon as you find out
for yourself
that the Kingdom
of Heaven
is in the mind
abroad and
within you.

* Matthew 6:33
— Luke 12:31

God is all mind,
all substance;
subjective
and objective.

Grace is a
  finer activity
    of the mind
than we normally
    experience.

It is like
  the waves
    in water
that a dropped
  pebble makes.

It is a thought
    before it is
        thought,
    that meets
        no resistance.

It is like
a snowflake
falling,
and does not collide
with another.

It is a universal law
that works
on the principle of:
what you are
is what you
will be
and do.

If you were
        a bird
    you would
        build a nest
in such and such
        a way;
    and you would
        fly to the south
            when winter comes
and to the north
        in the summer.

It is like the flow
    of a river
        that goes down hill
            and not up.

It works for those
who are in
complete trust
that it will,
and even for
those who
are untrusting.

It is your future
   extending out before you
      if you let it
         and do not interfere.

Doubts and fears
set up another
process
that brings
extinction
to the original idea.

In the latter case
we start
over again
after experiencing
a lesson.

Grace is the mind
in action
toward a perfection
already perfected.

It will eliminate
the karma
of our mistakes.

It is the healer
of those
who never were
sick.

It is your life
    as it was
        meant
           to be.

You find grace
in the eyes
of God —
in the image
compounded
of him and her.

And by his word:
. . . . *Let us make*
man
in our image,
after our
likeness : . . . .
                    — *Genesis I:26*

So God created
man in his own
image,
in the image of God
created he him;
male and female created he them.
                    — *Genesis I:27*

A holy temple even today
of grace
and love.

I like to think of <u>man</u>
as short
for the manifestation
of God —

but man alone
cannot,
even in the broadest
sense,
represent God.

Only the male and female
in infinite variety
can give
the perfect image
of that
which is the
Creator.

And this must
    include the darkness
    as well as the light.

She is the virgin
        descending
    out of Heaven
with a "down to earth"
        conception
of the mind,
giving free forms
to the mind's
own
articulation.

All we need to do is
to appreciate
the mind —
to know how
divine it is.

And we may or may not
spell divine
with a capital *D*
when we know
that consciousness
is the child or product
of the mind.

Which, though it
might fall,

rises

.... and, "*lo, I am with you*
alway . . . ."
— *Matthew 28:20*

The oneness ,
    of mind
      is its cause
and support.

Consciousness is the child
or product of the mind,
but
the mind itself
has gone
into its
making.
Therefore it is not
something other
than itself
but is
itself —
the mind,
in an unlimited
perspective.

To comprehend this
would bring about
the immaculate
conception
of anything
we are looking
at.

There is either an
immaculate
conception
or a
misconception.

A misconception
is no
conception
at all.

When we open
        our mind
        and put up
no resistance,

the Lord himself
        will give us
                a sign
of the presence
of mind
in everything
and everywhere.

All is purely
spiritual.

All exists in
the spirit
of one mind.

What do we do with
all our
misconceptions?

Nothing!

They simply drop
away
in the light
of truth.

This is where illness
and death
must go.

Get out your own paper
and pen
when there is a riddle
to be solved;

the spirit of your question
will be your
guide.

There are no walls
to tear down,
no bridges to cross,
no lack of
information,
no spirit of a loved one
missing.

They have been trying
for eons
to get our attention.

Lift up the eyes
that are blind.

Open the ears
that have been closed.

And prove or
disprove
these words
for
yourself.

www.ingramcontent.com/pod-product-compliance
Lightning Source LLC
Chambersburg PA
CBHW022011080426
42733CB00007B/562